108 N
S

VIJAYA KUMAR

Sterling Paperbacks

STERLING PAPERBACKS
An imprint of
Sterling Publishers (P) Ltd.
A-59, Okhla Industrial Area, Phase-II,
New Delhi-110020.
Tel: 26387070, 26386209; Fax: 91-11-26383788
E-mail: mail@sterlingpublishers.com
ghai@nde.vsnl.net.in
www.sterlingpublishers.com

108 Names of Shiva
© 2004, Sterling Publishers Private Limited
ISBN 978 81 207 2025 1
Reprint 2005, 2009, 2011

Printed in India

Printed and Published by Sterling Publishers Pvt. Ltd.,
New Delhi-110 020.

Preface

Lord Shiva is the quintessence of infinite wisdom, the source of sound and the Vedas, the bestower of boons. It is not possible to comprehend His grace through the intellect, but it can be perceived through the heart. He is the Lord of the three worlds.

Following the tradition of celebrating the holy names of God, we have chosen 108 names, signifying the 108 beads in a rosary.

The chanting of God's name evokes in us a religious fervour, and helps us to focus on the Almighty.

Vijaya Kumar

Shiva

ॐ श्री शिवाय नमः

The Auspicious Lord

Shiva is pure bliss, who controls everything and whom none can control. He is the primordial male and female energies. One is absolved of all sins when one chants Lord Shiva's name.

Maheshwara

ॐ श्री महेश्वराय नमः
The Grand Lord

Lord Shiva is the Supreme Ruler, the Ultimate God. As the source of all knowledge, it is only through sincere devotion that He can be attained.

Shambhu

ॐ श्री शंभवे नमः

The Giver Of Prosperity

The most benevolent and auspicious Lord, Shiva is the repository of great wealth and prosperity. He is ever generous and kind to His devotees, showering them with His blessings.

Pinaki

ॐ श्री पिनकिने नमः

The Holder Of the Bow Pinaka

Lord Shiva, bow in hand, is the Creator, Destroyer and Sustainer of the three worlds. His great bow is made of Sumeru Mount, the bow-strings of the body of the snake lord, Vasuki, and the fiery arrow was graced by Lord Vishnu.

Shashishekhara

ॐ श्री शशिशेखराय नमः
With Moon On His Hair

The crescent moon is an adornment in Lord Shiva's matted hair. Hence, He is also called Induchooda – Shashi and Indu both mean the moon. The moon was given refuge in Lord's Shiva's mattted hair when the former was under a curse.

Vamadeva

ॐ श्री वामदेवाय नमः
The Lovely Lord

The five-faced Mahesha or Mahadeva looks enchanting and magnificent, seated on His mount, Nandi. With His body radiating fragrance and brilliance, He looks grand and handsome in His loveliness.

Viroopaksha

ॐ श्री विरूपाक्षाय नमः

With An Eye On The Forehead

Lord Shiva is of infinite vision and His eyes are shaped like the lotus, with the third eye located on the forehead. These eyes represent the three aspects of nature – sattva, rajas and tamas.

Kapardi

ॐ श्री कपर्दिने नमः

Having Matted Hair

Lord Shiva's hair is thickly matted together and gathered above His forehead into a coil. Lord Shiva, with his matted hair, intercepted river Ganga's descent from Lord Vishnu's feet from heaven.

Neelalohita

ॐ श्री नीललोहिताय नमः

The Blue-Complexioned Lord

The auspicious visaged and blue-complexioned Shiva shines with the brilliance of a billion suns, radiating rays of power and love upon everything.

Shankara

ॐ श्री शंकराय नमः
The Granter Of Happiness

'Sham' means welfare and happiness, and 'kar' means bringer. Lord Shiva or Shankara, bestows peace, happiness and bliss on all his devotees.

Shoolapani

ॐ श्री शूलपाणये नमः
Having A Trident

Lord Shiva wields a three-pronged trident, denoting that He combines in His person the three attributes of the Creator, the Destroyer and the Regenerator.

Khadvangi

ॐ श्री खड्वाँगिने नमः

With Missile Khadvangin In Hand

The only Protector and Master of the three worlds, Lord Shiva, with His missile, destroys the enemies and provides succour to His noble disciples. He is the one who pierced the eye of the God Bhag (Bhrigu).

Vishnuvallabha

ॐ श्री विष्णुवल्लभाय नमः
The Spouse Of Vishnu

When Vishnu appeared in the form of a beautiful maiden to destroy the demon who had acquired an unusual boon from Shiva, He completely overwhelmed the demon by His beauty and brought about his downfall. Lord Shiva too fell for the beautiful Mohini and made her His spouse.

Shipivishta

ॐ श्री शिपिविष्टाय नमः

Possessing Special Powers

Lord Shiva, who is the embodiment of knowledge and wisdom, and whose nature is bliss, is the Possessor of special powers that make Him truly Supreme.

Ambikanatha

ॐ श्री अम्बिकानाथाय नमः

The Spouse Of Ambika

Lord Shiva is the beloved consort of Ambika (Uma or Parvati). Together they form the Eternal Couple, she being His Shakti or life-force.

Shreekanttha

ॐ श्री श्रीकंठाय नमः

Coloured Neck

The blue-throated Nilakanttha, Lord
Shiva is resplendent in all His glory,
with snakes garlanding around His
glorious neck.

Bhaktavatsala

ॐ श्री भक्तवत्सलाय नमः
Fond Of Devotees

The Great Lord Shiva, the Lord of the Trinity, is the Spiritual Teacher and Guide. He is Truth and His devotees adore Him, as He is also fond of His devotees.

21

Bhava

ॐ श्री भवाय नमः

The Source Of The Universe

Lord Shiva, by His indescribable power, Maya, creates the universe through His own will or imagination. His pure existence is the cause for the manifested world.

Sharva

ॐ श्री शर्वाय नमः

The Remover Of Sins

Lord Shiva is the Destroyer of all that is evil and sinful. Man has to keep fighting against evil in order to merge with the One. And the Lord will help destroy this evil if man will but make the effort.

Trilokesha

ॐ श्री त्रिलोकेशाय नमः

The Lord Of The Three Worlds

As the Creator of the three worlds, Lord Shiva is Omniscient and Omnipotent, beyond all attributes. It is out of His favour that all objects in the world are illuminated.

Shitikanttha

ॐ श्री शितिकंठाय नमः

Having A White Neck

When Lord Shiva, to save the world, swallowed the poison that emerged with the churning of the Ocean of Milk, his neck turned blue, but with the application of ash, it changed to white again.

Shivapriya

ॐ श्री शिवाप्रियाय नमः

Fond Of Parvati

Lord Shiva and Goddess Parvati form the Eternal Perfect Couple. He is fond of his beautiful consort, who is the daughter of the mountains.

Ugra

ॐ श्री उग्राय नमः

The Furious Lord

The fierce consuming wrath of Lord Shiva overwhelms His enemies, thus vanquishing them. His fury, in the form of a great flame from His third eye, dispels gloom.

Kapardi

ॐ श्री कपर्दिने नमः

With Matted Hair

Lord Shiva's matted hair holds the sacred river Ganga, the power and source of all movement in life. His thickly matted hair is gathered above His forehead forming a coil.

Kamari

ॐ श्री कामारये नमः
The Destroyer Of Kama

Kama's love arrows struck Lord
Shiva while He was mourning the
loss of Sati, as a result of which He
was captivated by Parvati. So to
punish Kama, the lord of love, Lord
Shiva incinerated him with fire
shooting forth from His third eye.

Andhakasurasoodhana

ॐ श्री अंधकासुरसूधनाय
नमः

The Slayer Of Andhaka

The Great Lord of power and strength, wielder of a trident and a thunderbolt, is the slayer of the dreaded demon, Andhaka, who had caused terror amongst the gods.

Gangadhara

ॐ श्री गंगाधराय नमः
The Holder Of Ganga

When the river Ganga gushed forth
from Vishnu's feet, Lord Shiva used
his matted locks to break the force of
the flow. Hence, he is marred as the
one who held river Ganga to break
the flow.

Lalataksha

ॐ श्री ललाटाक्षाय नमः

With Third Eye On The Forehead

The Omnipotent and Omniscient One has an eye in the forehead which is the window to the past, present and future. The moon, the sun and the fire are His eyes that are all-knowing and all-pervading.

Kalakala

ॐ श्री कालकालाय नमः
One Who Frightened Yama

When Sati, Shiva's wife, attended her father's yajna in spite of not being invited and then in humiliation abandoned her corporeal frame, a greatly angered Lord Shiva frightened Yama, the god of death, threatening him to death.

Krupanidhi

ॐ श्री कृपानिधिये नमः
The Bounty Of Compassion

The Great, Compassionate God of the poor, the downtrodden, and the miserable, is an unseen influence. He is Hara, the remover of obstacles, worries, troubles and enemies.

Bheema

ॐ श्री भीमाय नमः

Lord Who Is Strong Like Bheema

The sturdy, blue-necked Shiva, with a sinuous body dazzling like gold, is strong like Bheema, and He grants strength to His devotees.

Parashuhasta

ॐ श्री परशुहस्ताय नमः

The Wielder Of Axe

Lord Shiva wields the axe, gifted to him by the grace of Parashuram, destroying all egos and arrogance, and burning down all that is evil.

Mrugapani

ॐ श्री मृगपाणये नमः
The Holder Of Stag

Lord Shiva destroyed the sacrificial fire of Dalesha, wherein the fire escaped to the sky in the form of a stag. Lord Shiva captured this stag and held it in his hand.

Jatadhara

ॐ श्री जटाधराय नमः
With Matted Hair

Lord Shiva, the blue-necked Nilakanttha, with His matted hair, sports the river Ganga on His locks. The waters of river Ganga were intercepted by Lord Shiva who used His locks to break the force of the flow of Ganga.

Kailasavasi

ॐ श्री कैलासवासिने नमः

One Who Lives On Mount Kailash

Lord Shiva, the great ascetic, is known for His austerities. He lives on Mount Kailash and is Head of the gana or group of beings, gods, and sages.

Kavachi

ॐ श्री कवचिने नमः

The Armoured One

The thousand-eyed Lord of the
spirits wields a bow and arrow, a
trident, a rattle — all significant
symbols indicating the Supreme Self,
the Changeless Reality around which
all the terrestrial changes take place.

Katthora

ॐ श्री कठोराय नमः
One Who Is Very Strong

The Great Lord of power and strength, Lord Shiva wields a trident, a bow, and a thunderbolt. He is invincible, and is also the Destroyer of Tripura and other great demons.

Tripurantaka

ॐ श्री त्रिपुरांतकाय नमः
The Slayer Of Tripura

Lord Shiva is the Destroyer of the demon Tripura and his three cities. His fiery arrow, blessed by the grace of Lord Vishnu, vanquished and killed the terrible demon and burnt the cities to ashes.

Vrushanga

ॐ श्री वृषांगाय नमः
The Holder Of Stag

When Daksha's sacrificial fire was destroyed by Shiva, the fire escaped in the form of a deer in the sky. But Lord Shiva captured it and held it aloft in His hand to mark His victory.

Vrushabharooddha

ॐ श्री वृषभारूढ़ाय नमः

One Who Is Mounted On A Bull

The Great Lord of the three worlds, astride the bull, His famous mount Nandi, is lordly in His splendour and glory. The bull, representing the libido of man, is kept in check by Lord Shiva when He rides it.

Bhasmoddhoolita Vigraha

ॐ श्री भस्मोद्धूळित विग्रहाय नमः

Sprinkled Ash On Body

Lord Shiva, the Austere Ascetic who has matted hair, is the Lord of sacrifices. He possesses healing remedies, and with ashes sprinkled on His body He also embodies purity.

Samapriya

ॐ श्री सामाप्रियाय नमः

The Lover Of Samaveda

Lord Shiva, the Source of all knowledge, the Originator of sound, and of the Vedas, loves the Vedas, especially the Samaveda.

Swaramaya

ॐ श्री स्वरमयाय नमः
The Lord Of Musical Notes

Lord Shiva, from whom emanated the sound, is the Lord of music. He represents Nada, the sound and the evolution of the universe.

Trayimoorti

ॐ श्री त्रयीमूर्तये नमः
The Lord Of The Trinity

As Lord of the Trinity — Vishnu,
Brahma and Mahadeva — Lord
Shiva is the Lord of the three worlds.

Aneeshwara

ॐ श्री अनीश्वराय नमः
The Lord Of All

Lord Shiva, who is phaseless, auspicious, perfect, unborn, is the Lord of all, the root cause of all creation, and also its destruction.

Sarvagna

ॐ श्री सर्वज्ञाय नमः

The God Of All Knowledge

Lord Shiva is the embodiment of bliss that accrues by gaining knowledge. He is a great Ascetic and the most erudite Scholar, whose magnificent opulence is forever sung by Narada and other sages in the form of hymns.

Paramatma

ॐ श्री परमात्मने नमः
The Ultimate

The Supreme Lord of the three worlds is without any beginning or end. He is second to none and beyond comparison. He is the Pious One and the Ultimate.

Somasuryagnilochana

ॐ श्री सोमसूर्याग्नि लोचनाय नमः

With Moon, Sun And Fire As Eyes

The auspicious-visaged Lord Shiva has a third eye, which adorns His forehead, along with the moon. The wide-eyed Lord's three eyes are the sun, the moon and the fire, representing infinite vision.

Havishi

ॐ श्री हविषे नमः

One Who Gulped Poison

When the Ocean of milk was churned, a deadly poison also emerged amongst other things. This poison was drunk by Lord Shiva in compassion to save the world. This is the reason why Lord Shiva's throat had turned blue with poison.

Yagnamaya

ॐ श्री यज्ञमयाय नमः
The Sacrificial Fire

The resolute, profound and austered
Lord of sacrifices, Lord Shiva, is
Himself the Sacrificial Fire which is
lit to propitiate the gods and invoke
their blessings.

Soma

ॐ श्री सोमाय नमः

One Who Is Like The Moon

The red-eyed, blue-necked, fair and subtle-bodied Lord Shiva is undisturbed by any activity. Like the moon, He is eternally calm and watchful.

Panchavaktra

ॐ श्री पंचवक्त्राय नमः
The Five-Faced God

This is a form of Shiva in which He is represented with five faces. He is an embodiment of all that ensures the welfare of all. He is all-knowing, all-seeing, and fully aware of everything.

Sadashiva

ॐ श्री सदाशिवाय नमः

The Ever Auspicious God

Ishwar, Mahadeva, the Lord of the three worlds, the cause of creation, auspicious and changeless, is Sadashiva, the God that ever was and ever will be, without any beginning or end.

Vishweshwara

ॐ श्री विश्वेश्वराय नमः
The Lord Of The Universe

Lord Shiva is the Supreme Brahman
without any attribute or form. He is
Manifest and Unmanifest. He is
Existence, Knowledge and Bliss. As
the Lord of the universe, He causes
dissolution of the three worlds.

Veerabhadra

ॐ श्री वीरभद्राय नमः
The Most Valiant One

Lord Shiva, the Supreme Trinity, is the Supreme Leader of the three worlds. He is the Lord of the baser beings, the ghosts, goblins and lesser beings of the nether world.

Gananatha

ॐ श्री गणनाथाय नमः
The Master Of The Ganas

He is the Supreme Lord of the Lords, of the gods and celestial beings, of the three worlds. The ganas or celestial beings pay obeisance to Him and meditate upon Him, seeking His blessings for self-enlightenment.

Prajapati

ॐ श्री प्रजापतये नमः
Lord Of All Beings

Lord Shiva, by whom the whole world is manifest, and ultimately coalesces with Him only, is the Lord of all beings. He is the Creator, the Destroyer and the Regenerator.

Hiranareda

ॐ श्री हिरणरेदसे नमः

One Who Shines Like A Diamond

Lord Shiva is the Cause of all illumination, blazing and shining like a diamond with the brilliance of a thousand suns.

Durdasha

ॐ श्री दुर्दशाय नमः

Visible To People In Distress

When one is afflicted by sorrows and remembers Lord Shiva, He is visible to them in their distress, an indication of His granting them peace and serenity.

Gireesha

ॐ श्री गिरीशाय नमः
Mountain Lord

Lord Shiva, who holds the sacred river Ganga in His hair, is the Lord of the hills and mountains. Dweller of Mount Kailash, He is most bountiful and auspicious.

Girija

ॐ श्री गिरिजाय नमः

Spouse Of Girija

Beside Lord Shiva reposes His
beautiful, lotus-like consort, Girija or
Parvati or Uma. She is the graceful
daughter of the lofty mountains. He
is ever happy to please His shakti or
energy life-force, Parvati.

Anagha

ॐ श्री अनघाय नमः

Faultless

The blue-necked Shiva has innumerable forms. He is the root cause of the world and is the light manifest. He is beyond the decay of bodily stages and ignorance, without beginning and end. He is faultless and perfect.

Bhujangabhooshana

ॐ श्री भुजंगभूषणाय नमः
Adorned With Snakes

The blue-necked, three-eyed Shiva is
clasped by snakes, denoting the
endless cycle of recurring years. The
snakes adorn his neck, matted hair
and ears.

Sarga

ॐ श्री सर्गाय नमः
Extraordinary Deity

Lord Shiva, the One Infinite Reality, is an extraordinary Deity. He is thousand-eyed, with the third eye on his forehead. His blue neck, matted locks, and ash-covered body symbolise the Divine Form.

Giridhanvi

ॐ श्री गिरिधंविने नमः

Holder Of Mountain That Was Transformed Into A Bow

As Lord of the hills and mountains, Lord Shiva uprooted a mountain to transform it into a bow for vanquishing an obnoxious demon.

Giripriya

ॐ श्री गिरिप्रियाय नमः
Fond Of Mountains

Making Kailash his abode, Lord Shiva is a carefree reveller, who loves to wander on the mountains. His spouse Parvati, seated beside Him on Mount Kailash, worships Him most reverently.

Kruthavasa

ॐ श्री कृतवाससे नमः

Wearer Of Tiger Skin

Lord Shiva, the intelligent, the strong, the most bountiful, is resplendent in His tiger-skin attire, shining like a luminous moon. The tiger skin lends austerity to His divine form.

Puraradha

ॐ श्री पुराराधये नमः

Worshipped By Celestial Beings

Lord Shiva is most benign and compassionate, heaping happiness on His subjects. He is the Form of Eternal Bliss through whom happiness radiates.

Bhagavati

ॐ श्री भगवते नमः

The Ultimate

Lord Shiva, the Ultimate, is Self-existent, beyond the senses or illusion. He is the Self-luminous Truth, the Supreme God and Divinity.

Bramathadhipa

ॐ श्री ब्रमथाधिपाया नमः

Lord Of The Ganas

Lord Shiva, the Magnificent and Auspicious Lord, is Eternal. He is the Lord of the *Ganas*, the celestial beings, who worship Him fervently.

Mrutyunjaya

ॐ श्री मृत्युंजयाय नमः
Conqueror Of Death

Lord Shiva is the Conqueror of death, who can alter the course of destiny. He is the antidote for those who suffer in this worldly life. What destroys age is time, and as the Ruler of time, He is the Lord of destruction.

Sookshamatanu

ॐ श्री सूक्ष्मतनवे नमः
Subtle-Bodied

Lord Shiva is subtle-bodied, being Maya Himself. Fair as the snowy Himalayas, radiant like the brilliance of many suns, resplendent in all His glory, Shiva is the Abode of all.

Jagadvyapi

ॐ श्री जगद्व्यापिने नमः

Pervades The Universe

Lord Shiva pervades the whole universe. He is Inconceivable and Incomprehensible, but ever present in all ages and times, filling all vast spaces.

Jataguru

ॐ श्री जतगुरवे नमः
Music Teacher

As the Divine Music Teacher of all lords, Lord Shiva embodies all memory and knowledge. He is the Spiritual Teacher of the three worlds, and the Abode of all learning.

Vyomakesha

ॐ श्री व्योमकेशाय नमः
With Hair Touching The Space

Lord Shiva's matted hair is gathered together in a coil high above His forehead, the coils touching space, representing Him as the Lord of wind, Vayu, significant of the subtle form of breath.

Mahasenajanaka

ॐ श्री महासेनजनकाय नमः

Father Of Mahasena (Skanda)

Lord Shiva is the Father of Skanda or Kartrikeya, the dark-complexioned son of Uma. When the demon Taraka wrought havoc and distressed the gods, He sent the six-faced Kartikeya to slay the demon.

Charuvikrama

ॐ श्री चारुविक्रमाय नमः
Conqueror Of Beauty

Lord Shiva, the Divine Symbol of rhythm and sound, is the Giver of joy, and Conqueror of beauty. He embodies spectral beauty that lures everyone to Him.

Rudra

ॐ श्री रुद्राय नमः

The Ultimate Cause

The word 'Rud' connoting misery is attributed to Lord Shiva for he dispels misery. By conferring knowledge on the unfortunate miserables, He relieves them of misery and pain.

Bhootapati

ॐ श्री भूतपते नमः
Lord Of The Ghosts

He is the Ultimate of all spirits, the
Supreme Leader of nether world. He
is the Ruler of that which has been
synonymous with ghosts.

Sthanu

ॐ श्री स्थाणवे नमः

Immovable

Shiva, the intelligent, the strong and the bountiful, is the rock-like, immovable and everlasting Lord, who ever remains lighted in His Super Realm.

Ahirputnya

ॐ श्री अहिर्पुत्न्याय नमः
Lord Of All Things

Lord Shiva is the All-powerful
Supreme Divine Being, who is
pristine, formless, and the Performer
of amazing deeds. He is the Lord of
all things – animate and inanimate.

Digambara

ॐ श्री दिगम्बराय नमः

Who Dons Directions As Dress

The five-faced Shiva uses the
directions — East, West, North and
South – as His attire, embodying all
forms of learning and senses.

Ashttamoorti

ॐ श्री अष्टमूर्तये नमः
Eight-Faced

Lord Shiva is also known as the eight faced god, facing the four directions as well as North-east, North-west, South-east and South-west– ie, he is all-seeing, pervading the whole cosmos.

Anekatma

ॐ श्री अनेकात्मने नमः

Beloved Of Numerous

Lord Shiva, the Mine of all virtues, the Redeemer from mundane existence, is of lofty fame, ever revered by great sages, gods and other beings.

Satvika

ॐ श्री सात्त्विकाय नमः

Soft-Natured

Lord Shiva, the Supreme Almighty, is soft-natured and full of noble virtues. Many hymns and adulations are sung by His devotees in praise of His soft nature.

Shuddhavigraha

ॐ श्री शुद्धविग्रहाय नमः
Chaste Deity

The Great Lord Shambhu or Shiva is phaseless and auspicious. His pure body is anointed with sandalwood paste, and His fragrance pervades the three worlds.

Shashvata

ॐ श्री शाश्वताय नमः

Eternal

The Omniscient and Supreme Lord Shiva, without attributes and forms, without beginning or end, is all-pervading and eternal, beyond imagination.

Kantthaparashu

ॐ श्री कण्ठपरषवे नमः
All Praise For The Lord

The beings of the three worlds sing the glory of Lord Shiva who is Perfect Bliss and the Infinite Ocean of Knowledge.

Aja

ॐ श्री अजाय नमः

Invincible

Lord Shiva, who has no beginning or end, creates the entire world as Lord Brahma, sustains it as Lord Vishnu, and finally destroys the entire creation as Lord Shiva. He dwells in all the realms.

Pashavimochaka

ॐ श्री पाशविमोचकाय नमः

Detacher Of Attachments

Lord Shiva, personifying knowledge and wisdom, liberates man from worldly desires, so that he can transcend them and seek salvation.

Mruddha

ॐ श्री मृढ़ाय नमः

Granter Of Happiness

Lord Shiva is most benign and compassionate, showering happiness on His subjects. He is the Form of Eternal Bliss from whom happiness radiates.

Pashupati

ॐ श्री पशुपतये नमः
Lord Of The Animals

The most benevolent, compassionate
and kind Lord is Pashupati, Lord of
the animals. He protects them and
gives them succour, removing their
troubles and giving them shelter.

Deva

ॐ श्री देवाय नमः
Lord

Lord Shiva is the Creator and Destroyer of the three worlds. He is the Ultimate, the All in All, the Supreme Lord, who is beyond measure.

Mahadeva

ॐ श्री महादेवाय नमः

The Great Lord

Lord Shiva is the Supreme God, pervading all, but stationed in the single syllable 'Aum'. He is the Great Atman, the Lord of lords, and there is no greater Atman than Him.

Avyaya

ॐ श्री अव्ययाय नमः
Imperishable

The Invincible Lord, who has no equal or comparison, is the Infinite, Supreme God. He is without beginning and is Infinite. He creates, sustains and destroys, and is the Ruler of Time.

Hari

ॐ श्री हरये नमः

Destroyer Of Sins

As the Creator, the Sustainer and the Destroyer, Lord Shiva is not different from Lord Vishnu or Lord Brahma. He is the Annihilator, the Scorcher of all wrongs, sins and evils.

Pooshatantapi

ॐ श्री पूशतंतपिते नमः

Lord Vishnu

Lord Shiva, in His various forms, is Vishnu who desires sincere worship from all His devotees. The Bright and Happy One is formless, yet manifests Himself in various forms.

Avyagra

ॐ श्री अव्यग्राय नमः

Without Worries

Lord Shiva, embodying an ocean of calmness and bliss, is without worries, unruffled, calm and collected, ever wakeful and composed that make Him so dignified and divine.

Dakshadhwarahara

ॐ श्री दक्षध्वरहराय नमः

*Destroyer Of Daksha's
Sacrificial Fire*

Lord Shiva, who was not invited to
the yajna performed by Daksha,
Uma' father, destroyed the sacrificial
fire, signifying that the worshippers
are not different from Him – He is in
them all.

Hara

ॐ श्री हराय नमः

Withholder Of Sins

As a Killer of sins and a Deliverer who heals while He destroys, Lord Shiva is the Master of life and death. As the destroyer of sins, He forgives all those who are penitent and seek His forgiveness and blessings.

Baganetrapi

ॐ श्री बगनेत्रपिते नमः
Having Third Eye

Lord Shiva is the three-eyed Supreme Deity, the third eye adorning the centre of His forehead. This is the inner eye of wisdom. All multiplicity burns down when Lord Shiva opens this third eye.

Avyaktha

ॐ श्री अव्यक्ताय नमः

Invisible

Lord Shiva is the primordial Lord, who is the Creator as well as the Destroyer. He is Maya, who is His power, potency and strength, being invisible and unmanifest.

Sahastraksha

ॐ श्री सहस्त्राक्षाय नमः
Thousand-Eyed

The thousand-eyed Shiva is Infinite, Imperishable and Omniscient. His vision is infinite, beyond past, present and future, all-pervading and all-knowing.

Sahastrapati

ॐ श्री सहस्त्रपते नमः

Having Thousand Forms

Lord Shiva has endless forms and endless beauty. In His thousand forms, His heads are a multitude, and He is the Self in all. Many and mighty are His forms, but He is hidden.

Apavargaprada

ॐ श्री अपवर्गप्रदाय नमः

Granter Of Auspicious Things

The Great Benefactor that He is, Lord Shiva grants one the power to shed his ego and merge into Him, for He is the Granter of auspicious things.

Ananta

ॐ श्री अनंताय नमः

Infinite

Lord Shiva, the Ultimate Power who destroys and regenerates the cosmos, is the Infinite Source of all, from whom the creation emanated and whose fount is infinite and limitless.

Taraka

ॐ श्री तारकाय नमः

Promoter

The Eternal, Unchangeable and Immutable Shiva establishes and promotes the rule of law and order whenever necessary. Nothing moves or transpires without His Will.

Parameshwara

ॐ श्री परमेश्वराय नमः
Lord Supreme

Lord Shiva is universally manifest.
The whole world is instinct with His
presence, as He is all-pervading, the
Source of all light through whom
everything else is illuminated.